SUICIDE BOMBERS

FIGHTING TERRORISM

David Baker

Rourke
Publishing LLC
Vero Beach, Florida 32964

www.rourkepublishing.com

PHOTO CREDITS: p. 32: AFP/Getty Images; p. 37: Yasser Al-Zayyat/AFP/Getty Images; p.
24: Odd Andersen/AFP/Getty Images; p. 36: Louai Beshara/AFP/Getty Images; p. 5: Adek
Berry/AFP/Getty Images; p. 30: Robert E. Curran/AFP/Getty Images; pp. 8 (Tech. Sgt. Cedric
H. Rudishill), 31, 33: Department of Defense; pp. 6, 7: Chris Fairclough/Chris Fairclough
Worldwide Ltd; p. 34: Ramzi Haidar/AFP/Getty Images; pp. 10, 12: Keystone/ Getty Images;
p. 4: Mary Evans Picture Library; p. 27: Robert Nickelsberg/Getty Images; p. 38: Miguelito
Parcero/AFP/Getty Images; p. 13: PhotoDisc; p. 26: David Rubinger/Time life Pictures/Getty
Images; p. 16: Yaakov Saar/GPO via Getty Images; p. 15: STR-AUSAF NEWS
PAPERF/AFP/Getty Images; p. 43: Transportation Security Administration; p. 18: Pedro
Ugarte/AFP/Getty Images; pp. 14 (Senior Airman Richard M. Heilman), 19 (Staff Sgt. LeeAnn
Sunn-Wagner), 41 (Tech. Sgt. Cedric H. Rudishill): U.S. Air Force; p. 20 (Spc. Katherine H.
Roth): U.S. Army; pp. 22 (t) (Lance Cpl. Thomas D. Hudzinski), 22 (b) (Master Sgt. Buzz
Farrell): U.S. Marine Corps; pp. 40 (Chief Petty Officer Kevin Elliott), 42 (Photographer's
Mate 1st Class Michael Moriatis): U.S. Navy

Title page picture shows the Khobar Towers in Saudi Arabia following the 1995 suicide
bombing.

Produced for Rourke Publishing by Discovery Books
Editor: Paul Humphrey
Designer: Ian Winton
Photo researcher: Rachel Tisdale

Library of Congress Cataloging-in-Publication Data

Baker, David, 1944-
  Suicide bombers / by David Baker.
     p. cm. -- (Fighting terrorism)
  Includes index.
  ISBN 1-59515-487-6
  1. Suicide bombers--Juvenile literature. 2. Suicide bombings--Juvenile
literature. I. Title. II. Series.
  HV6431.B335 2006
  363.32--dc22
                                        2005028010

Printed in the USA

TABLE OF CONTENTS

Chapter One

The Ultimate Sacrifice

Terrorism has been a part of our world for a very long time. Reasonable people who want to change things usually choose peaceful ways to wage their campaign. Some, however, choose to injure, kill, and destroy as a way to

Terrorism has been around for a long time. This picture shows the assassination of the Archduke Ferdinand of Austria-Hungary in June 1914, an event that sparked World War I (1914-1918).

force others to accept their demands. Some select terror as a means of combining two things: a desire to pressure people into submission to their will and a means of destroying things they do not agree with.

Sometimes these uncontrolled desires are linked to fanatical beliefs fueled by **extremist** views. Sometimes they are linked to interpretations of religious beliefs that give terrorists **justification** for what they do. Either way, they are unlawful uses of force and a terrible way to express a belief.

These Muslims in Indonesia are peacefully demonstrating against the war in Iraq. Most people choose peaceful demonstrations to express their views, but terrorists use kidnapping, hijacking, and mass murder.

No major religious group accepts the right of one human to kill another for personal gain or to destroy life for an idea. Yet there are some who choose to re-interpret religious beliefs in a way that will support their own cause. In doing so they bend the

Many people who carry out suicide bombings claim it is an instruction of their Islamic faith. This is not so. The **Prophet** Muhammad provided believers with direct instructions on how to react to what is perceived as an **aggressive** act against them: "Do not be people without minds of your own, saying that if others treat you well you will treat them well, and that if they do wrong you will do wrong. Rather accustom yourselves to do good if people do good, and not to do wrong if they do evil."

truth; the only way to combat that is to go to the origin of their claims and test them against facts.

Terrorists who plant bombs, injure people, and destroy property are condemned by decent citizens in every country. They, and those who encourage others to commit similar acts of terrorism, are outlawed by every religion in the world

A young Muslim reads the Koran, the holy book for Muslims. Nowhere in the Koran does it justify the killing of innocent people.

today. Where do they get their justification? To understand that is to understand the terrorist and a very old quotation from the Bible **exhorting** people to "know thine enemy" is a good reason to start. It is only possible to fight terrorism by fully understanding the causes and the motivations of these men and women who commit acts of unspeakable horror.

The world in which we live has a rapidly expanding population, which means we will all have to tolerate widely different views to survive. People travel a lot more than they used to and encounter unfamiliar beliefs, new

Multicultural New York City. We live in a world today where people of many colors and faiths live together, usually in harmony. Many terrorists, though, seek to spread discord throughout our communities.

ideas, and diverse patterns of faiths and religions. What are we to make of these differences? Should we be afraid of them? The only way we can understand extreme acts such as mass murder is by separating fact from fiction. There is no better place to start than by going to the very origin of suicide bombing and the claims made by those who support it.

Chapter Two

The Price for Life

One of the most memorable and terrible moments of recent time was the suicide bombings of the World Trade Center Twin Towers in New York City and the Pentagon building near Washington, D.C., together with the fourth passenger plane brought down short of its intended target by heroic passengers. That was on September 11, 2001, a day that people around the world remember with horror. More than 3,000 people from many countries were killed in those terrible events.

The events of 9/11 were carried out by suicide bombers who had no sense of guilt in killing as many people as quickly as possible and in losing their own lives as a result. The memory of that day will live on, but it was not a unique event. The reality is that suicide bombers have been around for as long as different ideas have been in conflict with each other and countries have made war, and that is a very long time.

Today's suicide bombers attack innocent people. The act itself seems **barbaric**, but giving up a life for a cause has a long history. Throughout time people have rushed to defend their countries, their families, or beliefs that they are passionate to see grow and be universally accepted. For these causes many have knowingly and deliberately killed themselves in the process. Passion and loyalty can drive people to perform outstanding feats of heroism and foolishness, not always as a planned response but as a rapid reaction to a threat.

From ancient times dedicated professional fighting men and women have frequently given their lives for a cause they believe in. Fanatical and sworn defenders of a faith or a ruler have moved ordinary people to give up their lives for the religious

(Opposite) An aerial view of the Pentagon taken on September 14, 2001, just three days after fanatical suicide bombers destroyed part of the building with a passenger plane full of people.

belief, or the powerful leader, they follow. This is usually associated with a passionate commitment to a cause or an individual, and it can blind people to reason and logic.

Throughout history religions have taught the existence of a supreme God and a life after death. Total belief in that view has led many to lose their lives in **fruitless** attempts to influence the outcome of a battle or take the lives of the enemy along with their own. In doing so, they believe they gain favor in the idea of life after death. The use of the human body as a weapon capable of bringing death to the enemy in human sacrifice is recorded in the ancient texts of Chinese and Japanese warriors.

The earliest known instances of suicide bombings go back to the 11th century, when the Assassins, the disciples of the Persian ruler Alamut, carried out suicide attacks on a neighboring fortress town. As recently as World War II (1939-1945),

The plane of a Japanese kamikaze suicide bomber lies burning on the deck of an allied aircraft carrier during World War II.

Japanese suicide bombers hit warships in the Pacific in a futile attempt to turn back U.S. naval forces. They did so believing their mission was divinely inspired.

In that war, after the attack on Pearl Harbor, Hawaii, on December 7, 1941, the Japanese swept south to occupy all countries down to the seas separating Indonesia from Australia and as far west as the border with India. In four years of intensive battles, the Japanese were driven back, as one by one the Pacific islands were liberated.

In the final months of the war the Japanese were running short of materials due to intensive U.S. bombing of Japan's weapons production plants. To intensify attacks against aircraft carriers and other warships, they recalled an old Japanese story known as **kamikaze**, which means "divine wind." The story goes that in the 13th century the invading fleet of the Mongol leader Kublai Khan was turned back by a divine wind, thus saving Japan from a terrible onslaught.

Recent **archaeological** evidence proves the story true. Japanese pilots relived the kamikaze by diving their bomb-laden planes onto the decks of U.S. aircraft carriers, killing themselves

Religion sometimes divides whole nations. In 1948, the Indian sub-continent was divided into Hindu India and Muslim Pakistan and much bloodshed followed. This picture shows a riot in Calcutta, India.

in the process while hoping to sink the warship. These suicide attacks were said to guarantee a good place in the **afterlife**, and many went willingly to their deaths.

It is difficult for most of us to understand that kind of logic. Many people believe in life after death, but they are unable to accept that any deed involving the killing of others, especially innocent people, can ever give them grace in Heaven. The concept of an afterlife is common throughout most religions of the world. It can often be a powerful influence in how desperate people behave. The use of religious texts and writings to justify extreme acts of war or aggression is common throughout history.

For centuries, religion has been used by Christians, Jews, Muslims, Hindus, and others to justify terrible acts of aggression.

It is only when we ourselves become the targets for extremism that we fully realize the destructive way in which not only the victims but also the **perpetrators** are killed.

However, there are many countries and people around the world who feel they have no voice and must use whatever means they can to express their fears or frustrations. Like Japanese kamikaze airmen in World War II, suicide bombers are pushed to carry out their mission by those who drive them and influence their actions.

In time of war it is assumed that our fighting men and women will make every effort to defend what they believe is a right and just cause. We have democratic government to make sure that

Congress meets in the U.S. Capitol building. It is the seat of our government and a symbol of our democracy. It is this democracy that some terrorists are determined to undermine.

An American servicewoman checks a truck in Saudi Arabia. Osama bin Laden and his Al Qaeda group object to the presence of American forces in Saudi Arabia because the country contains some of the holiest places for Muslims.

no one individual, or group of people, can seize power and take control against our will. Of course, we cannot all have everything we want in a just and fair society. That is why we elect representatives to speak for us and make decisions, and if we don't like what they do we can change them every two or four years.

We agree to abide by the majority decision, and we have **electoral** control over who represents us. It is a fair way of getting our voices heard on an equal basis, uniting the poor and the rich, the successful and the unsuccessful.

Not every country in the world is like this. Many countries do not practice **democracy**, and their people have no way of getting their voices heard. They are ruled by leaders who control power, whether they are good at it or not. They are without democratic representation, and their leaders have no responsibility to account to the people for their actions. This breeds a level of desperation that can result in acts of violence. It can also lead to frustration about the way their country is run.

Osama bin Laden, the terrorist leader of Al Qaeda, **protests** against western influence in Saudi Arabia and has taken a path of murder and violence to get his message across and bring pressure on those who run the country. In other cases desperate people make protests against foreign troops on their land; Palestine is an example of this. The Palestine Liberation Organization, or PLO, grew out of frustration with the presence of Israeli settlements in Palestine, and suicide bombers have brought death and destruction to many innocent people in the region.

It is to organizations such as Al Qaeda and the PLO that suicide bombers are attracted, some volunteering their lives,

Osama bin Laden is head of the Al Qaeda terrorist group.

Yasser Arafat was the head of the PLO and a notorious terrorist. He later became the head of the Palestinian Authority and made some attempt to make peace with the Israelis. For this he was awarded the Nobel Peace Prize in 1994.

FACT FILE ★

An important part of **counterterrorism** is to encourage democracy in **dictatorships** and countries ruled by leaders who inherit their **totalitarian** power. This was an important part of the reason given by the administration of President George W. Bush for attacking Iraq and removing Saddam Hussein from power. With free elections people are able to decide their own future; this choice disarms terrorists by taking away their reason for violence.

with others being forced to carry out such acts while their loved ones are held hostage. Some suicide bombers have second thoughts and cannot go through with their actions.

There have been several examples in Iraq and in Palestine where young boys have been told their mothers or sisters will be killed unless they carry out a suicide attack. Family loyalties are high among people of these regions, and the guilt they accept for not carrying out their actions is a lifelong burden.

Chapter Three

The Human Bomb

There are various ways a suicide bomber works, and a variety of reasons why they are part of the terrorist's arsenal of weapons. Suicide bombers are recruited by two different types of people, those who organize terror attacks and those who will lead others to suicide. Plans to carry out suicide attacks usually come from senior leadership in a terrorist organization. Suicide bombers rarely act independently or without some backup support. In this way they are easier to detect because sometimes it is possible to **pre-empt** the preparations made by these organizations.

Tapping telephone conversations or listening to radio messages sent by mobile or satellite phones allow specialists to predict converging activity. Terrorist organizations with money and resources such as those available to Al Qaeda allow the group to plan thoroughly. Paradoxically, they leave more trails by which they can be detected. When they are detected, individuals are watched and their movements are tracked.

Some organizations are only loosely controlled. Iraqi groups resisting U.S. troops in that country are not directly connected

An Israeli man looks at a destroyed bus at the scene of a twin suicide bombing of two buses in the southern Israeli town of Beersheva, August 31, 2004. At least 15 people were killed, as well as two bombers, and more than 80 were wounded in the attacks.

to organizations like Al Qaeda in the same way, but they do have the support of the main terrorist groups. Al Qaeda is against the presence in Muslim countries of non-Islamic foreigners in positions of authority and control. The group fought to get the Russians out of Afghanistan during the 1980s, and today they fight to get non-Islamic influence out of Middle Eastern countries. Al Qaeda has common ground with the terrorists in Iraq and provides active help and support.

Usually, when a suicide bomber is selected from a small group appointed to carry out such acts or is accepted as a volunteer, he or she is given a mission and is trained in the basic techniques needed to achieve maximum effect. Most volunteers have a strong motivation, and the majority of volunteers have to be restrained from rushing at their enemy without preparation.

A member of the 1st Cavalry Division searches through the rubble after two explosions ripped through a market place in Baghdad, Iraq, on October 14, 2004. The explosions left Americans and local civilians dead or injured.

Car bombs have proved to be a favored weapon for terrorists in Iraq. Here, smoke fills the air after a car bomb was detonated in the parking lot of an Iraqi police station in Baghdad, December 4, 2004.

The majority of those directed to carry out an attack show all the signs of conflict between a desire to kill and achieve glory in the afterlife and the natural instinct to survive. Only a few turn back without going through with the planned attack.

Preparation can in some circumstances take many months. These are hard-line **fanatics**, cool and calm under pressure and with only one intention: to kill as many people as they can. Such were the bombers who carried out the attacks of 9/11, converting airliners into **missiles**. In fact there are three categories of suicide bomber, two of which use forms of transportation to carry their bombs.

The most dramatic category is the bomber who uses airplanes as weapons with no additional explosive carried other than the energy of the plane itself and the fuel it carries. Fortunately these are rare, although 9/11 demonstrated their most dramatic use to bring down the Twin Towers of the World Trade Center in New York City.

Other forms of transportation used without explosives include small boats propelled into ships to blow them up, the force of the impact causing an explosion. This too is not a popular form of attack but it does require a suicide mission.

The second category of bombers uses trucks, SUVs, cars, or vans to carry explosives to a site where vehicles left abandoned would be immediately suspect. The bombers know they can only reach the target and **detonate** the explosives by driving

These metal ball-bearings found by Marines in Baghdad, Iraq, April 12, 2003, were to be used in the making of suicide bombing vests. The small photo shows a home-made trigger that could set off a suicide bomber's explosives.

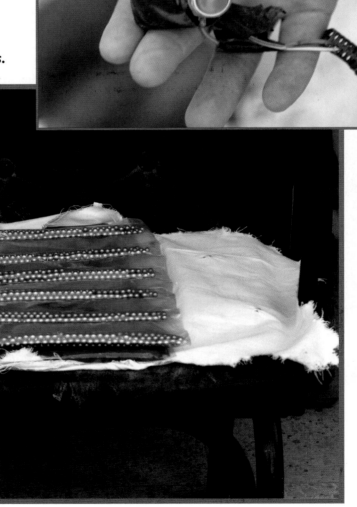

up and doing it themselves without pause or hesitation.

Targets for car bombs detonated in suicide missions include densely congested areas, guarded sites, government buildings, gas stations, and other places where the bomb can explode with maximum death and destruction.

The third category is the bomber who carries explosives attached to his or her body. All that is needed are the packages of explosive, a detonator, and a method of triggering the device —usually electrically activated from a hand-held button switch.

Explosives can be powder, solid, or plastic and are packed inside a molded bag strapped to the body, usually under the long, loose garments worn by most people in the hot, dry atmosphere of the Middle East.

This type of suicide bomber is usually assisted by a group of support terrorists who ensure that the bomber's path is clear and unimpeded. There are at least four other people involved with every bomber who uses body-mounted explosives. Many of the bombers are indoctrinated to the task by emotional, religious, or financial bribes.

Some people believe that radical Islamic preachers can stir up trouble among young Muslims. Abu Hamza al-Masri was arrested in London in August 2004 under Britain's 2004 Terrorism Act. He is also wanted in the United States.

There have been several instances where family members are looked after financially after the suicide bomber has done his or her deed. The understanding that their loved ones will be looked after is a **palliative** for the unsure and the uncertain facing death. Religious blackmail involves misrepresentation of texts by extremist clerics rewriting ancient books to deliver a violent and abrasive message.

Just how easy it is to twist and distort the exact words of religious text is seen in the way basic statements are changed. There are particular references in Islamic text to the virtue in fighting **oppression**. "He who gives his life for an Islamic cause will have his sins forgiven and a place reserved in paradise," says the Muslim holy book, the **Koran**. This is declared by some clerics to **legitimize** suicide bombings. However, the prophet Muhammad has written that "harming innocent bystanders, even in times of war, is forbidden."

The political and religious differences between Palestinians and Israelis turn the region into a favored recruiting ground for bombers. Some journalists have conducted a survey in Palestine and claim that 76 percent of Palestinian adults in the West Bank and the Gaza Strip approve of suicide bombings.

Although not all are successful, young recruits and volunteers are always available and encouraged by their parents to commit their lives as suicide bombers. Most are devout followers of religious dogma and spend several hours a day in prayer and contemplation for the task ahead.

The profile of a typical Palestinian suicide bomber is not what many people would expect. Of the 100 bombers since the early 1990s, about 83 percent are single. Almost all are under the age of 30, and two-thirds are under 23. Perhaps surprisingly, three out of four have academic qualifications or a high school education. These young men and women are well informed,

A slum district of the Gaza Strip. This part of the Middle East is peopled mostly by Palestinians but was, until recently, occupied by Israeli forces. It has become a fertile breeding ground for terrorists.

The parents of a suicide bomber proudly show the photograph of their daughter, Ayat, who blew herself up in a Jerusalem café in July 2002. Ayat's radical views had been encouraged by her mother.

highly committed in what they do, and studious. Most come from families who are proud that their sons or daughters give their lives in this way. Parents are often eager to talk to journalists, to get wide recognition, and to publicize the name of their dead son or daughter. All are convinced that they and their son or daughter will achieve a special place in heaven.

Because the level of acceptance within the local community gives general support to suicide bombers, there is a network of support between the families with members who have chosen that way to die.

Chapter Four

The Modern Age of Bombers

The modern era of suicide bombings really began in 1983, when the Shi'ite terrorist organization called Hezbollah began a rain of more than 50 attacks in Lebanon. Shi'ite **guerrillas**

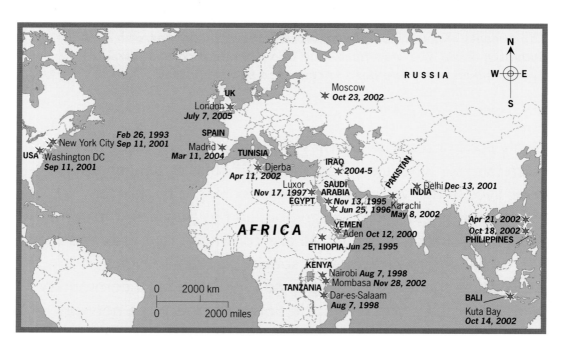

This map shows where some of the major terrorist attacks were carried out.

specially trained and supported by Iran killed 299 people, of whom 242 were American, in simultaneous operations in Beirut, Lebanon. Hezbollah's reputation soared in the wake of these attacks, a reputation that increased with every fresh atrocity.

Word spread throughout the world, and while civilized and reasonable human beings were appalled, extremists were impressed. New organizations inspired by Hezbollah began their own spate of bombings.

First the Tamil Tigers fighting for an independent Tamil state in Sri Lanka adopted Hezbollah tactics. The first Tamil suicide bombings started in 1987, and since then more than 200 such attacks have taken place. They were spectacularly successful in killing several hundred people. They became the only terrorist organization to succeed in **assassinating** two heads of state by suicide bombing.

In May 1991, India's Prime Minister Rajiv Gandhi was killed by a Tamil bomb during an election tour in Madras. Then, in May 1993, President Premadassa of Sri Lanka was one of 23 people killed by a

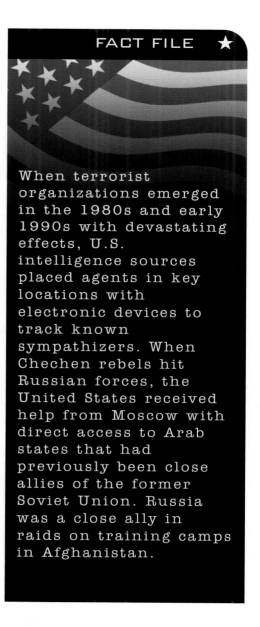

FACT FILE ★

When terrorist organizations emerged in the 1980s and early 1990s with devastating effects, U.S. intelligence sources placed agents in key locations with electronic devices to track known sympathizers. When Chechen rebels hit Russian forces, the United States received help from Moscow with direct access to Arab states that had previously been close allies of the former Soviet Union. Russia was a close ally in raids on training camps in Afghanistan.

The funeral of India's prime minister, Rajiv Gandhi in May 1991. Gandhi had been killed by Tamil Tiger terrorists.

The Khobar Towers in Saudi Arabia following the June 25, 1996 suicide bombing. The facility housed U.S. service members and served as the headquarters of the U.S. Air Force's 4404th Wing.

suicide bomber. Only by a narrow margin did the Tamils fail to kill Chandrika Kumaratunga, the Sri Lankan President, in December 1999.

During the 1990s two Egyptian terrorist organizations carried out suicide attacks, one in Croatia and the other at the Egyptian embassy in Karachi, Pakistan. But it was only when Al Qaeda began to form into a major terrorist organization with several thousand followers that major attacks began in earnest.

The destruction caused by the bombing of the U.S. embassy in Nairobi, Kenya, in August 1998.

Two simultaneous suicide bombings against the U.S. embassies in Nairobi, Kenya, and Dar-es-Salaam, Tanzania, killed 224 people and injured several thousand. Later, in a suicide attack, apparently by Al Qaeda, two bombers blew themselves up in a boat in Aden harbor alongside the USS *Cole*, killing 17 soldiers.

By 2000 Osama bin Laden had begun a major export operation, taking terror to new places. Militant **separatists** fighting against the Russian army were recruited to the successful training methods of Al Qaeda and began using volunteers for suicide missions. To date more than 100 Russian soldiers have died in at least seven attacks.

The USS Cole *is here pictured just after the October 12, 2000 terrorist attack, which left 17 U.S. Navy personnel dead.*

A Syrian Kurdish woman member of the PKK at a rally in support of Ocalan, the leader of the terrorist movement, in March 2004.

Another group that embraced the suicide bomber was the Kurdish PKK, a so-called secular Islamic movement demanding Kurdish **autonomy**. Of the 21 attacks the group attempted in 1995 and 1996, the PKK was successful in 16, killing 20 people and wounding more than 100. Inspired by their **charismatic** leader Ocalan, the PKK stopped its suicide bombings after his arrest and death sentence in 1999.

The most consistent pressure from suicide bombers has taken place against the state of Israel. Since 1993 there have been well over 300 suicide bombing attempts against Israeli settlements in Palestinian territories and against military occupation. Just over half of the more than 300 attempts have been successful, but the success rate has declined from 70 percent through 2000 to slightly more than half since then.

More than two-thirds of suicide bombings in the region are carried out by four groups of terrorist organizations. These are Hamas (42 percent of attacks), Palestinian Islamic Jihad (28 percent), Fatah (27 percent), and the Popular Front for the Liberation of Palestine, or the PFLP (3 percent). Formed in 1987, Hamas is pledged to the elimination of the Jewish state of Israel and consists of a military wing, an underground movement for suicide attacks, and a political wing.

Palestinian Islamic Jihad began as a small group of militant fundamentalists from the Gaza Strip during the 1970s. It seeks to conduct a holy war for the destruction of Israel and the establishment of an Islamic Palestinian state. It sees the United States as its enemy because of its support for Israel. It even operates a network inside the United States to carry out attacks.

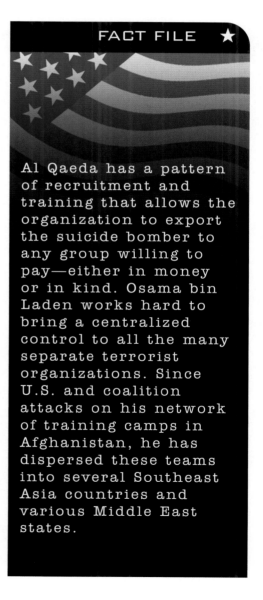

FACT FILE ★

Al Qaeda has a pattern of recruitment and training that allows the organization to export the suicide bomber to any group willing to pay—either in money or in kind. Osama bin Laden works hard to bring a centralized control to all the many separate terrorist organizations. Since U.S. and coalition attacks on his network of training camps in Afghanistan, he has dispersed these teams into several Southeast Asia countries and various Middle East states.

The PFLP had an unusual beginning, emerging from a communist group led by George Habash. Founded in 1967, it supported a revolution in all Arab states to root out foreign involvement in internal affairs. It actively contributes suicide

George Habash, the leader of the PFLP from 1967 until 2000.

Al Qaeda terrorist fighters training in Afghanistan in June 2001. Many Palestinian suicide bombers trained at camps like these before returning home to carry out their deadly missions.

bombers and regularly maintains links with other groups including Al Qaeda.

Al Qaeda has persistently tried to work its way into the Palestinian troubles to take over control of mass murder and terrorist attacks using suicide bombers. Its members are well trained and have a strong base from which to export terror. Al Qaeda has attempted to export bombers to Palestine, and the PLO has used bombers trained in Al Qaeda camps in Afghanistan and other countries.

Chapter Five

Prevention and Cure

For all the horror and misery that have been created by Al Qaeda and similar terrorist organizations, it is reassuring to know that many attacks have been prevented and disrupted. These include an attempt to assassinate Pope John Paul II during his visit to Manila in 1994/95. Another attempt, to kill President Bill Clinton during a visit to the Philippines in 1995, was similarly thwarted. In 1995 a plan to bomb 12 U.S. Trans-Pacific airline flights was intercepted and stopped, and a bomb planted at the Los Angeles airport was discovered and defused.

Constant vigilance and the certain knowledge that suicide bombers are the most extreme of fanatics and the most persistent of terrorists encourage continuous efforts to track down volunteers and recruits. Methods now being developed through the Department of Homeland Security make it easier for U.S. citizens to go about their business in the knowledge that security forces are getting much better at stopping these fanatical murderers.

Technology available today and increased resources, which bring more money and people to attack prevention, seem to help stop the numbers of bombings. With a global intelligence network there has never been a better chance to build a defense against organized suicide attacks.

In reality, however, there will never be a defense against the fanatic with a belt of explosives and a death wish. Security systems and a human screen protecting vital assets are all parts of sustained efforts to contain the threat. But nothing can ever exceed the security that comes from converting those who feel

(Opposite) Pope John Paul II watches a local Philippine dance during his tour of the Philippines. There was an attempt to assassinate the Pope while he was in the Philippine capital, Manila, during this tour.

A U.S. Navy officer uses a mirror to examine the underside of a truck during a security check near the Kuwait-Iraq border at Camp Navistar, Kuwait, on March 8, 2005.

desperation in finding a sense of purpose and to instill a desire to build a purposeful life.

While prevention is a vital part of anti-terrorism, the prospect of providing a cure for this particularly murderous form of attack is possible. Increasingly, security and attack prevention specialists are learning to understand the psychology of the suicide bomber.

It is possible, say some experts in terrorist behavior, to profile a likely suspect and to compile a list of potential bombers.

Increasingly, through lists discovered in Afghanistan training camps, **sleeper cells** of bombers waiting to strike are being discovered. Specialists in negotiating with extremists and hostage

President George W. Bush and Defense Secretary Donald Rumsfeld at a press conference following the September 11, 2001, suicide bombings. The Bush administration's response to the terrorist outrage was swift. Within months U.S. and coalition forces were attacking Al Qaeda training camps in Afghanistan.

Sailors carry a wounded comrade to safety during a simulated suicide bomb exercise in Chesapeake, Virginia. Soon these sailors may face the real thing in Iraq.

takers say the best way to cure the desire to carry out such acts is to persuade all groups that such action is not a winning strategy.

The general public must have a resolute determination not to be terrorized into submitting to the demands of extremist groups. Moreover, it must be clear that these events achieve nothing sought by their perpetrators.

Countering suicide attacks requires astute political handling of the basic problems that give rise to the attacks. It also requires a **proactive** military and intelligence force that can act against the perpetrators swiftly and without compromise. The consequence of not tackling the extreme problem of the bomber is unacceptable. That consequence is to surrender to blackmail and terrorism, which, in a democracy, we must never do.

All passengers, whatever their ages, may be subject to searches when passing though U.S. airports. Only in this way can we be sure that the events of September 11, 2001 will never be repeated.

Glossary

afterlife: life after death (for some religions)

aggressive: when a person, group, or country shows fierce or threatening behavior toward others

archaeological: learning about the past by digging up remains of things

assassinate: to murder an important person such as a president

autonomy: when a country or region has the right to govern itself

barbaric: very cruel behavior

charismatic: someone who is charismatic has a lot of charm and inspires devotion in others

counterterrorism: the act of preventing terrorism

democracy: a way of governing a country in which the people are able to elect a government

detonate: set off an explosion

dictatorship: a government run entirely by one person

electoral: describes anything concerning an election

exhorting: strongly encouraging someone to do something

extremist: someone who has extreme beliefs or takes extreme actions

fanatic: someone who is wildly enthusiastic about something such as a belief, a cause, or an interest

fruitless: unsuccessful or useless

guerrilla: a member of a small, unofficial army fighting an official army

hypnotism: the act of hypnotizing someone, or putting them into a trance

justification: when a reason is given to an action to prove it is necessary

kamikaze: a suicide attack during World War II in which a Japanese plane full of explosives was crashed into an enemy target

Koran: the sacred text of Islam

legitimize: to justify something or make it lawful

missile: an object or weapon that is thrown or fired at an enemy target

oppression: the use of power in a cruel way

palliative: something that relieves pain or a problem without dealing with the main cause

perpetrator: the person who is responsible for carrying out an action

pre-empt: to take an action in order to stop something from happening

proactive: doing something in advance in order to prevent possible difficulties

prophet: a person who predicts what will happen in the future

protest: to strongly and publicly object to something

separatist: someone who supports the separation of a group of people or region from a larger group or country

sleeper cell: a place where terrorists may live in a country for many years before committing acts of terrorism

totalitarian: a system of government that requires complete control over a state

Further Reading

Binns, Tristan. *The CIA (Government Agencies)*. Sagebrush, 2002

Binns, Tristan. *The FBI (Government Agencies)*. Sagebrush, 2002

Brennan, Kristine. *The Chernobyl Nuclear Disaster (Great Disasters)*. Chelsea House, 2002

Campbell, Geoffrey A. *A Vulnerable America (Lucent Library of Homeland Security)*. Lucent, 2003

Donovan, Sandra. *How Government Works: Protecting America*. Lerner Publishing Group, 2004

Gow, Mary. *Attack on America: The Day the Twin Towers Collapsed (American Disasters)*. Enslow Publishers, 2002

Hasan, Tahara. *Anthrax Attacks Around the World (Terrorist Attacks)*. Rosen Publishing Group, 2003

Katz, Samuel M. *Global Counterstrike: International Counterterrorism (Terrorist Dossiers)*. Lerner Publishing Group, 2004

Katz, Samuel M. *Targeting Terror: Counterterrorist Raids (Terrorist Dossiers)*. Lerner Publishing Group, 2004

Katz, Samuel M. *U.S. Counterstrike: American Counterterrorism (Terrorist Dossiers)*. Lerner Publishing Group, 2004

Margulies, Phillip. *Al-Qaeda: Osama Bin Laden's Army of Terrorists (Inside the World's Most Infamous Terrorist Organizations)*. Rosen Publishing Group, 2003

Marquette, Scott. *America Under Attack (America at War)*. Rourke Publishing LLC, 2003

Morris, Neil. *The Atlas of Islam*. Barron's, 2003

Owen, David. *Hidden Secrets: A Complete History of Espionage and the Technology Used to Support It*. Firefly Books Ltd, 2002

Ritchie, Jason. *Iraq and the Fall of Saddam Hussein*. Oliver Press, 2003

Websites to visit

The Central Intelligence Agency:
www.cia.gov

The Department of Defense:
www.defenselink.mil

The Department of Homeland Security:
www.dhs.gov

The Federal Bureau of Investigation:
www.fbi.gov

The U.S. Air Force:
www.af.mil

The U.S. Army
www.army.mil

The U.S. Coast Guard:
www.uscg.mil

The U.S. Government Official Website:
www.firstgov.gov

The U.S. Marine Corps:
www.usmc.mil

The U.S. Navy:
www.navy.mil

The U.S. Secret Service:
www.secretservice.gov

The White House:
www.whitehouse.gov

Index